SECURITY CAMERAS

101

A Beginner's Guide to Choosing, Installing, and Using a Camera System for Your Home or Business

Steven C. Ewers

TABLE OF CONTENT

Introduction

Security Cameras 101 is a comprehensive guide that covers everything you need to know about choosing, installing, and using a security camera system for your home or business. Whether you want to deter crime, monitor your property, or enhance your safety, this guide will help you find the best cameras for your needs, install them properly, and manage them effectively.

The manual is segmented into four primary parts:

Understanding the Importance of Security Cameras: This section explains the benefits of having a surveillance system, the types of security cameras available, and the frequently asked questions about security cameras.

Choosing the Right Security Cameras: This section helps you determine your security needs, the types of cameras to consider, and the factors to consider when choosing cameras.

Installing Security Cameras: This section guides you through the process of finding the ideal locations for your cameras, positioning and angling them, powering and connecting them, setting up the video recorder, configuring the camera settings, setting up remote access, and testing the system.

Monitoring and Managing Your Surveillance System: This section shows you how to monitor your cameras live, record and store the footage, receive notifications and alerts, analyze the recorded footage, access and control your system remotely, and maintain your system.

The guide also provides tips and best practices for using security cameras, such as privacy and legal considerations, lighting and visibility, regular maintenance and upkeep, integration with other security measures, training and user access management, and more.

Security Cameras 101 is a valuable resource for anyone who wants to learn how to set up and use a security camera system for their home or business. It is written in a clear and concise manner, with helpful illustrations and examples. It is based on the latest research and expert advice from the security industry. By following this guide, you will be able to enhance the security and safety of your property with confidence.

Importance of home security and the role of security camera systems

Home security is important because it can protect your property, your loved ones, and your peace of mind from potential threats such as burglary, vandalism, or intrusion. Security camera systems are one of the most effective ways to enhance your home security, as they can deter criminals, provide valuable evidence, offer remote monitoring capabilities, and increase home value, among others.

Some of the benefits of security camera systems are:

Crime Deterrent: Security cameras are recognized as an excellent deterrent to criminals, as they make them less likely to target your home or business. Studies have shown that indicators of increased security, such as outdoor surveillance cameras, were considered by most burglars when selecting a target.

Evidence Collection: Security cameras can record videos and sounds in great detail, which can help identify and convict criminals in case of a crime. The recordings can also help investigators understand how the events unfolded and who else might be involved.

Dispute Settlement: Security cameras can help resolve disputes between employees, customers, neighbors, or family members, as they can provide an objective and reliable record of what happened.

Remote Monitoring: Security cameras can allow you to check in on your property from anywhere, using your smartphone or computer. You can see a live feed of your home, receive notifications and alerts of any unusual activity, and control your system remotely.

Home Value: Security cameras can increase the value of your home, as they can make it more attractive to potential buyers or renters. They can also lower your insurance premiums, as they can reduce the risk of theft or damage1.

Security Cameras 101 is a comprehensive guide that covers everything you need to know about choosing, installing, and using a security camera system for your home or business. It is based on the latest research and expert advice from the security industry. By following this guide, you will be able to enhance the security and safety of your property with confidence.

Types of security camera systems

There are many types of security camera systems available for different purposes and settings. Here are some of the most common ones and their features:

Wired security camera systems: These systems use cables to connect the cameras to a central recording device, such as a digital video recorder (DVR) or a network video recorder (NVR). They are usually more reliable and secure than wireless systems, as they are less prone to interference and hacking. However, they also require professional installation and may be difficult to hide or relocate.

Wireless security camera systems: These systems use Wi-Fi or other wireless technologies to transmit the video signals from the cameras to a recording

device or a cloud storage service. They are easier to install and move than wired systems, as they don't need cables or drilling. However, they also depend on the quality and availability of the wireless network, and may be vulnerable to interference and hacking.

IP security camera systems: These systems use internet protocol (IP) to send and receive data over a network, such as a local area network (LAN) or the internet. They can be either wired or wireless, depending on the type of connection they use. They offer higher resolution and more features than analog systems, such as remote access, motion detection, and analytics. However, they also require more bandwidth and storage space, and may be more expensive than analog systems.

Battery-powered security camera systems: These systems use rechargeable batteries to power the cameras, eliminating the need for wires or outlets. They are ideal for locations where electricity is not available or convenient, such as outdoors or in remote areas. They are also easy to install and move, as they are usually wireless and compact. However, they also have limited battery life and may need frequent charging or replacement.

Floodlight security camera systems: These systems combine security cameras with bright LED lights that can be triggered by motion or sound. They are designed to illuminate and record the area around the cameras, as well as deter and scare away intruders. They are suitable for outdoor use, especially at night or in dark places. However, they also consume more power and may annoy neighbors or wildlife with their brightness.

Doorbell security camera systems: These systems integrate security cameras with doorbells, allowing you to see and communicate with visitors at your door. They can be connected to your smartphone or tablet, so you can monitor your door from anywhere. They can also record and store the footage of the visitors, as well as send you notifications and alerts. They are useful for enhancing your home security and convenience, as well as preventing package theft and unwanted solicitors.

Components of a security camera system (cameras, DVR/NVR, cables, etc.)

A security camera system consists of several components that work together to capture, process, and display surveillance footage. Here are the main components and their functions:

Cameras: These are the devices that capture the video and audio signals from the environment. They can vary in size, shape, type, and features, depending on the purpose and setting of the system. Some common types of cameras are wired, wireless, IP, battery-powered, floodlight, and doorbell cameras.

DVR/NVR: These are the devices that record and store the video and audio data from the cameras.

DVR is an acronym for digital video recorder, while NVR stands for network video recorder.

The main difference between them is that DVRs use analog signals and NVRs use digital signals. DVRs are compatible with analog cameras, while NVRs are compatible with IP cameras.

Cables: These are the wires that connect the cameras to the DVR/NVR and the power supply. They can be coaxial cables, Ethernet cables, or power cables, depending on the type of camera and system. Cables are essential for transmitting the signals and providing the power to the cameras.

Monitor: This is the device that displays the live or recorded footage from the cameras. It can be a computer screen, a TV, or a dedicated monitor. Monitors allow you to view and control your security camera system.

Data Storage: This is the device or service that stores the video and audio data for future use. It can be a hard disk drive, a solid state drive, a memory card, or a cloud storage service. Data storage is important for keeping a backup of your surveillance footage and accessing it remotely.

how to choose the right Choosing the right security camera system for your needs

Choosing the right security camera system for your needs can be a daunting task, especially with so many options and features available on the market. However, by following these steps, you can make an informed decision and find the best solution for your home or business.

Decide what parts of your home or business you want to protect: The first step is to identify the areas that you want to monitor with your security camera system. For example, you may want to cover the front door, the backyard, the garage, the office, the warehouse, etc. You should also consider the size, layout, and lighting conditions of each area, as well as the potential threats and risks that you want to prevent or detect.

Choose your power source: The next step is to decide how you want to power your security cameras. There are mainly two options: wired or wireless. Wired cameras use cables to connect to a power outlet and a recording device, while wireless cameras use batteries or solar panels to operate. Wired cameras are more reliable and secure, but they require professional installation and may be difficult to hide or relocate. Wireless cameras are easier to install and move, but they depend on the quality and availability of the wireless network and the battery life.

Determine your budget: The third step is to set a budget for your security camera system. The cost of a security camera system can vary depending on the number, type, and features of the cameras, as well as the recording device, the data storage, and the installation fees. You should also factor in the ongoing costs of maintenance, monitoring, and subscription services. You can find security camera systems for different price ranges, from less than $100 to over $1,000.

Pick the right features: The fourth step is to choose the features that you need or want for your security camera system. Some of the common features are:

Resolution: This is the quality and clarity of the video that the camera captures. Higher resolution means more details and better zooming capabilities, but it also requires more bandwidth and storage space. The standard resolution for security cameras is 1080p, but you can also find higher or lower resolutions depending on your needs.

Night vision: This is the ability of the camera to see in low-light or dark conditions. Most security cameras have infrared LEDs that emit invisible light to illuminate the area and capture clear images at night. The range and quality of the night vision can vary depending on the camera model and the ambient light.

Motion detection: This is the feature that triggers the camera to start recording when it detects movement in its field of view. This can help save battery life and storage space, as well as alert you of any suspicious activity. Some cameras also have advanced motion detection features, such as person detection, animal detection, or facial recognition, that can reduce false alarms and provide more accurate notifications.

Audio: This is the feature that allows the camera to capture and transmit sound, as well as enable two-way communication. Some cameras have built-in microphones and speakers that let you listen and talk to the people or animals in the camera's view. This can be useful for greeting visitors, scaring off intruders, or checking on your pets.

Field of view: This is the angle and area that the camera can see. A wider field of view means more coverage, but it may also result in more distortion and less detail. A narrower field of view means less coverage, but it may also provide more focus and clarity. The typical field of view for security cameras ranges from 90 to 180 degrees.

Storage: This is the feature that determines how and where the video and audio data from the camera are stored. There are mainly two options: local or cloud. Local storage means using a physical device, such as a hard drive, a memory card, or a USB flash drive, to store the data. Cloud storage means using an online service, such as Google Drive, Dropbox, or iCloud, to store the data. Local storage is more secure and accessible, but it has limited capacity and may be damaged or stolen. Cloud storage is more convenient and scalable, but it may require a subscription fee and an internet connection.

Consider your privacy: The final step is to think about the privacy and security implications of using a security camera system. While security cameras can help protect your property and loved ones, they can also pose risks to your personal information and data. Some of the privacy and security issues that you should be aware of are:

Hacking: This is the risk of unauthorized access to your security camera system by hackers or cybercriminals. They may be able to view, record, or manipulate your video and audio feeds, as well as access your personal data and network. To prevent hacking, you should use strong passwords, encryption, firewalls, and antivirus software, as well as update your firmware and software regularly.

Spying: This is the risk of unwanted or illegal surveillance by third parties, such as the government, law enforcement, employers, or neighbors. They may be able to monitor your activities, behavior, or conversations, as well as invade your privacy and rights. To avoid spying, you should follow the local laws and regulations regarding the use of security cameras, as well as respect the privacy and consent of others.

Sharing: This is the risk of exposing or leaking your video and audio data to the public or other parties, such as the media, social media, or advertisers. They may be able to exploit, misuse, or abuse your data, as well as harm your reputation or identity. To prevent sharing, you should be careful about who you grant access to your security camera system, as well as review the privacy policies and terms of service of the camera manufacturer and the cloud storage provider.

By following these steps, you can choose the right security camera system for your needs and enjoy the benefits of enhanced security and safety. For more information and tips on how to secure your home or business, you can check out these resources:

Preparing for installation (choosing camera locations, assessing power and connectivity requirements)

Choosing camera locations: You should choose the best locations for your cameras based on your surveillance needs and the layout of your property. You want to cover the most vulnerable and critical areas, such as entrances, exits, windows, driveways, porches, stairways, etc.

You also want to avoid placing the cameras in areas where they can be easily tampered with, blocked, or damaged, such as low heights, blind spots, or extreme weather conditions. You can use a diagram or a blueprint of your property to mark the potential camera locations and measure the distances between them.

Assessing power and connectivity requirements: You should also determine how you will power and connect your cameras to the recording device and the network. Depending on the type of cameras you have, you may need to run cables or use batteries or solar panels. You should also check the quality and availability of the wireless network or the internet connection in the camera locations, and see if you need any additional routers, extenders, or upgrades to handle the bandwidth and data transmission. You should also consider the cost and convenience of the power and connectivity options, and choose the ones that suit your budget and preferences.

By preparing for installation, you can ensure a smooth and successful setup of your security camera system and enjoy the benefits of enhanced security and safety.

Setting Up Your Home Security Camera System

Planning Your Surveillance: Prioritize your surveillance needs by creating a diagram of your home. Instead of monitoring every inch, focus on crucial areas like front and back doors, off-street windows, common spaces, driveways, porches, and stairways. Sketch a rough layout or use blueprints to identify optimal camera placements. Ensure there are no obstructions, allowing for the best possible views.

Choosing the Right Package: Opt for a bundled security system to save money and simplify the setup process. Essential components include 1-3 cameras, a digital video recorder (DVR), appropriate wiring (siamese and BNC cables), and power cords. For basic home security, go for a package with 2-3 outdoor cameras to monitor doors and a DVR with at least 3 days of recording time. If you're focusing on monitoring valuables or young children in a small room, 1-3 indoor wireless cameras streaming footage to your computer should suffice.

Individual Camera Purchase Option: Consider buying cameras individually once you determine the quantity required. The cost of a home surveillance system varies, ranging from a few hundred dollars to over a thousand. Prioritize camera selection based on your needs, and ensure the desired features are clearly labeled on the box. While purchasing components separately is an option, opting for a complete "surveillance set" is generally more cost-effective and easier to set up.

Wireless vs. Wired Considerations: Choose between wireless and wired cameras based on your preferences. Wireless cameras offer easy setup without drilling or running cables, but quality may diminish at greater distances from the receiver. For extensive coverage, opt for wired cameras, although many find wireless more convenient for installation.

Indoor or Outdoor Selection: Select cameras designed for their intended placement. Cameras not built for outdoor use may quickly deteriorate when exposed to rain and humidity, so choose accordingly.

Motion Sensing Efficiency: Opt for cameras equipped with motion sensing capabilities. These cameras record only when motion is detected, conserving space and energy by capturing footage only when activity is present.

Remote Viewing Benefits: Explore high-end cameras that allow remote viewing of footage on your phone or laptop from anywhere globally. This feature enables monitoring your property through a provided program or app.

Setting Up Recording and Monitoring: Acquire a Digital Video Recorder (DVR) to store and view your footage. The DVR consolidates video feeds and displays them on a monitor, typically a computer screen or small TV. DVRs come with various memory capacities, storing video ranging from hundreds of hours to one day's footage. When purchasing a complete surveillance set, the DVR is often included with the cameras.

Alternative Recording Devices: Consider Network Video Recorders (NVR) and analog recorders (VCRs), available for separate purchase. They function similarly to DVRs, using an internet signal (NVR) or blank tapes (VCR) for recording instead of a digital hard drive.

Pre-installation Equipment Testing: Ensure the functionality of cables, DVR, cameras, and monitor by testing each component before installation. This step ensures that all equipment works seamlessly together.

Method 2

Installing Your Camera

Choosing Optimal Camera Placement: Opt for a high, broad angle for your camera, typically from the corner where the ceiling meets the walls, offering the best perspective of the room. Ensure clear visibility of all entries and exits, placing the camera near a power outlet. For outdoor mounting, position the camera above 10ft to prevent easy tampering.

Wall Mounting Procedure: Securely mount your camera to the wall. While some cameras provide sticky pads for attachment, the safest long-term method is screwing the camera in. Though specific steps may vary, the general process includes:

Place the mount in the desired location.

Use a sharpie to mark the wall where each screw should go.

Use an electric drill to create a hole for each screw.

Hammer in any molding pins.

Screw the mount into the wall.

Adjust the camera to your preferred angle.

Powering Your Camera: Connect your camera to a power source using the provided power adapter. Most cameras come with an adapter that plugs into a standard wall socket. Insert the small, round end into the camera's power input and the other end into the outlet.

Adapter Replacement: If your power adapter is missing or damaged, reach out to the manufacturer for a replacement. Ensure proper functionality and connectivity before proceeding with the camera installation.

Connecting a Wired Camera to Your DVR:

Utilizing BNC Connections:

Link your wired camera to the DVR using a BNC (Bayonet Neill–Concelman) connection. BNC cables are straightforward—being identical on both ends, you plug them into the appropriate ports and secure them in place by turning a small nut at the end. Connect one end to your camera's "Output" and the other to an "Input" port on the DVR.

Identifying DVR Input:

Take note of the input port you've connected to; this is the input your DVR must be set to for viewing your camera's video feed.

BNC Adapter Option:

If your cable lacks a BNC connection, purchase a BNC adapter online or at a hardware store. This adapter slips onto the cable end, making it BNC compatible.

Linking Wireless Cameras to Your Computer:

For wireless cameras, install the provided software disc to view the feeds. Follow on-screen instructions, and ensure any small receiver connecting to your computer via a USB port is properly attached. If an IP address (e.g., 192.168.0.5) is provided, note it down for remote camera viewing through any web browser.

Connecting the Monitor to the DVR:

Attach the monitor to the DVR, often using a BNC cable. Some DVRs may also connect with HDMI or coaxial cables. Use your preferred connection, linking one end to the DVR's "Output" port and the other to the monitor's "Input."

Hook up as many cameras as your DVR has inputs; it will automatically record each installed camera. Take note of the input you've used, as this is the one you select to view your cameras.

Troubleshooting Connections:

Check that the camera, DVR, and monitor are powered on. Ensure secure cable attachments and select the correct inputs for your DVR and monitor. Some monitors display all cameras simultaneously, while others have "input" buttons for switching between cameras. Troubleshoot any connection issues as needed.

Method 3 of 3:

Centralizing Your Surveillance System:

Establishing a Central Hub: Create a central "surveillance hub" for wiring multiple cameras. Choose an easily accessible location where wires can be comfortably run from anywhere in the house. Suitable places include attics, offices, or near your internet router. This hub serves as the central point for bringing all camera feeds together to connect with your DVR. It's recommended to have only one DVR for all your cameras.

Effective Wiring with Siamese Cables: Use Siamese cables for efficient wiring. These cables consist of two attached cables—one for power and the other for video. This setup allows you to run a single wire for each camera. Siamese cables are commonly sold as RG59 or RG6. The braided red and black side handles power (red for positive, black for negative), while the cylindrical cable manages video, featuring either a BNC attachment or a coaxial cable at each end.

Power Supply Box for Multiple Cameras: Employ a power supply box to power multiple cameras through a single outlet. Available online and in hardware stores for $30-$50, these boxes simplify powering cameras close together or those not near an outlet (e.g., attic cameras). Connect cameras before powering the box and ensure it is of sufficient size to support all cameras, considering the number of outlets listed on the box.

Connecting Video Cables to DVR Ports: Attach each video cable to a separate DVR port. Your DVR has the capacity to handle multiple cameras simultaneously, enabling the recording of every room with a single box. Your monitor will display all cameras, or you can cycle through them using the "input" button on your DVR.

Concealing Your Cables:
Professional Cable Concealment: Achieve a polished, professional appearance by concealing your cables. Run wires through walls towards your surveillance hub for a seamless look. Prioritize understanding your wall layout and identifying any pipes, cables, or studs before initiating the wiring process. Drilling into the wall and threading cables

through open spaces, typically the attic, is the standard procedure.

Seeking Professional Assistance: If uncomfortable with wall drilling and cable installation, consider hiring a professional carpenter or handyman for cabling tasks. Ensure a tidy and discreet installation by using staples to secure cables to walls or baseboards.

Alternative Cable Concealment: Explore hiding cables under rugs, securing them with tape to prevent accidental tripping. This provides a visually clean setup without compromising safety.

Professional Home Security Installation: Alternatively, enlist the services of home security specialists for a custom system. Numerous security companies offer installation of cameras, motion sensors, and automatic emergency calling. While this option comes at a higher cost compared to DIY installations, it's ideal for those with larger houses, discomfort with wiring, or a desire for additional features like motion sensors and alarm systems. Well-known nationwide providers include ADT, LifeShield, Vivint, and SafeShield.

Connecting cameras to power and configuring network settings

To connect the cameras to the power source, you have two options: using power adapters or using PoE (Power over Ethernet) switch. Power adapters are simple devices that plug into the wall socket and provide 12V DC power to the cameras. PoE switch is a device that can provide both power and data to the cameras over a single Ethernet cable. PoE switch is more convenient and efficient, but it requires PoE compatible cameras and cables.

To configure the network settings of the cameras, you need to access their web interface using a computer or a mobile device. You can find the IP address of the cameras using a utility program from the camera's vendor, a network scanner app, or the Command Prompt program on your Windows computer. Once you have the IP address, you can enter it in your web browser and log in to the camera's web interface. There you can adjust the camera settings, such as resolution, frame rate, motion detection, and night vision. You can also set up the network settings, such as IP address, port forwarding, and DDNS.

System Configuration and Settings

Access the Camera System's User Interface in Security Camera System

A security camera system consists of one or more cameras that capture video and audio signals, and a recorder that stores and processes the data. The recorder may also have a built-in web server that allows users to access the camera system's user interface via a web browser. The user interface is a graphical interface that enables users to view live or recorded footage, configure settings, manage alerts, and perform other functions.

Prerequisites

To access the camera system's user interface, you need the following:

A computer or mobile device that has a web browser installed and is connected to the same network as the recorder.

The IP address of the recorder. The IP address is a unique identifier that allows devices to communicate over a network. The default IP address of most recorders is 192.168.1.108 or 192.168.1.109, but it may vary depending on the model and configuration. You can find the IP address of your recorder in the network menu inside the recorder's GUI interface, or by using a network scanning tool such as SADP or Angry IP Scanner.

The username and password of the recorder. The default username and password are usually "admin" and "12345", but they may have been changed by the installer or the user. You can find the username and password on a label on the top of the recorder, or by contacting the manufacturer or the installer.

Steps

To access the camera system's user interface, follow these steps:

Open the web browser on your computer or mobile device.

Type the IP address of the recorder into the address bar of the web browser and press Enter. For example, if the IP address of your recorder is 192.168.1.108, type http://192.168.1.108 and press Enter.

You will see a login interface that asks for your username and password. Enter the username and password of the recorder and click Login. Note: Some recorders may have an illegal login lock feature that blocks the IP address of the device after a certain number of failed login attempts. If this feature is enabled, you will need to wait for 30 minutes or disable the feature in the recorder's settings before trying again.

You will see the web interface of the recorder, which may look different depending on the model and software version of the recorder. The web interface usually has a menu bar on the top or the left side that contains various options such as Live View, Playback, Configuration, Maintenance, and Logout. You can click on these options to access different functions and settings of the camera system.

To view live or recorded footage from the cameras, click on Live View or Playback. You will see a grid of camera views that you can select, zoom, pan, tilt, or rotate. You can also control the playback speed, volume, and quality of the video. You can also take snapshots, record clips, or download footage to your device.

To configure settings such as camera parameters, network settings, storage settings, alarm settings, and user management, click on Configuration. You will see a list of submenus that allow you to adjust various aspects of the camera system. You can also update the firmware, restore the default settings, or backup and restore the configuration files of the recorder.

To perform maintenance tasks such as rebooting the recorder, checking the system status, viewing the logs, or diagnosing the network, click on Maintenance. You will see a list of tools that help you troubleshoot and optimize the performance of the camera system.

To log out of the web interface, click on Logout. You will see a confirmation message that asks if you want to log out. Click Yes to log out, or No to stay logged in.

Setting up user accounts and passwords In security Camera system

Setting up user accounts and passwords in security camera system is an important step to ensure the security and privacy of your video footage. Different camera systems may have different methods and interfaces for creating and managing user accounts, but the general steps are as follows:

Connect your computer or mobile device to the same network as the camera system's recorder.

Open a web browser and enter the IP address of the recorder in the address bar. You can find the IP address in the network menu of the recorder's GUI interface, or by using a network scanning tool such as SADP or Angry IP Scanner.

Log in with the default or existing username and password of the recorder. The default username and password are usually "admin" and "12345", but they may vary depending on the model and configuration of the recorder. You can also find them on a label on the top of the recorder, or by contacting the manufacturer or the installer.

Navigate to the user management menu of the recorder's web interface. The location and name of this menu may vary depending on the model and software version of the recorder, but it is usually under the configuration or settings section. You can refer to the user manual of the recorder or the manufacturer's website for more information and guidance on how to access the user management menu.

Click on the add user button or icon to create a new user account. You will need to enter a username, a password, a confirmation password, and a level or role for the new user. The level or role determines the permissions and privileges of the user, such as viewing live or recorded footage, configuring settings, managing alerts, and performing maintenance tasks. You can choose from predefined levels or roles, such as guest, operator, or admin, or customize the permissions for each user. You will also need to enter the admin password to confirm the changes.

Click on the save or OK button to create the new user account. You will see the new user account in the user list of the user management menu. You can edit or delete the user account by clicking on the corresponding buttons or icons next to the user name.

Log out of the web interface and log in with the new user account to test if it works correctly and has the desired permissions and privileges. You can also create more user accounts for different users or purposes following the same steps.

Adjusting camera settings (resolution, motion detection, night vision, etc.)

Adjusting camera settings in security camera system is a way to optimize the performance and quality of your video footage. Different camera systems may have different methods and interfaces for adjusting camera settings, but the general steps are as follows:

Connect your computer or mobile device to the same network as the camera system's recorder.

Open a web browser and enter the IP address of the recorder in the address bar. You can find the IP address in the network menu of the recorder's GUI interface, or by using a network scanning tool such as SADP or Angry IP Scanner.

Log in with the username and password of the recorder. The default username and password are usually "admin" and "12345", but they may vary depending on the model and configuration of the recorder. You can also find them on a label on the top of the recorder, or by contacting the manufacturer or the installer.

Navigate to the camera settings menu of the recorder's web interface. The location and name of this menu may vary depending on the model and software version of the recorder, but it is usually under the configuration or settings section. You can refer to the user manual of the recorder or the manufacturer's website for more information and guidance on how to access the camera settings menu.

Select the camera that you want to adjust from the list of connected cameras. You will see a preview of the camera view and a set of controls to adjust various settings. Some of the common settings that you can adjust are:

Resolution: This is the number of pixels that the camera captures in each frame. Higher resolution means more details and clarity, but also more storage space and bandwidth. You can choose from different resolution options, such as 4K, 1080p, 720p, etc., depending on the capability of your camera and recorder.

Frame rate: This is the number of frames that the camera captures per second. Higher frame rate means smoother motion, but also more storage space and bandwidth. You can choose from different frame rate options, such as 30 fps, 15 fps, 10 fps, etc., depending on the capability of your camera and recorder.

Bit rate: This is the amount of data that the camera compresses and sends to the recorder per second. Higher bit rate means higher quality, but also more storage space and bandwidth. You can choose from different bit rate options, such as 8 Mbps, 4 Mbps, 2 Mbps, etc., depending on the capability of your camera and recorder.

Motion detection: This is a feature that allows the camera to detect and record only when there is movement in the scene. This can save storage space and bandwidth, and also trigger alerts and notifications. You can enable or disable motion detection, and also adjust the sensitivity, area, and schedule of motion detection.

Night vision: This is a feature that allows the camera to capture clear images in low-light or dark conditions. This can be achieved by using infrared LEDs, starlight sensors, or color night vision technology. You can enable or disable night vision, and also adjust the brightness, contrast, and mode of night vision.

Adjust the settings according to your preference and need. You can use the preview to see the effect of the changes. You can also compare the settings of different cameras and apply the same settings to multiple cameras if you want.

Click on the save or OK button to apply the changes. You will see a confirmation message that the settings have been updated. You can also restore the default settings or reset the camera if you want.

Configuring recording schedules and storage options in security Camera system

Configuring recording schedules and storage options in security camera system is a way to control when and where the video footage is recorded and stored. Different camera systems may have different methods and interfaces for configuring these settings, but the general steps are as follows:

Connect your computer or mobile device to the same network as the camera system's recorder.

Open a web browser and enter the IP address of the recorder in the address bar. You can find the IP address in the network menu of the recorder's GUI interface, or by using a network scanning tool such as SADP or Angry IP Scanner.

Log in with the username and password of the recorder. The default username and password are usually "admin" and "12345", but they may vary depending on the model and configuration of the recorder. You can also find them on a label on the top of the recorder, or by contacting the manufacturer or the installer.

Navigate to the storage settings menu of the recorder's web interface. The location and name of this menu may vary depending on the model and software version of the recorder, but it is usually under the configuration or settings section. You can refer to the user manual of the recorder or the manufacturer's website for more information and guidance on how to access the storage settings menu.

Select the storage location of the video files. You can choose from different storage options, such as the internal hard disk drive (HDD) of the recorder, an external USB drive, a network attached storage (NAS) device, or a cloud storage service. You can also set the storage quota, format, and overwrite options for each storage location.

Navigate to the recording schedule menu of the recorder's web interface. The location and name of this menu may vary depending on the model and software version of the recorder, but it is usually under the configuration or settings section. You can refer to the user manual of the recorder or the manufacturer's website for more information and guidance on how to access the recording schedule menu.

Select the camera (channel) that you want to configure the recording schedule for. You can also enable or disable the recording schedule for each camera. You can choose from different recording modes, such as continuous, motion detection, alarm, or a combination of them. You can also customize the recording schedule by drawing time periods on a calendar or using predefined templates. You can also set the recording quality, resolution, frame rate, and bit rate for each recording mode.

Click on the save or OK button to apply the changes. You will see a confirmation message that the settings have been updated. You can also restore the default settings or reset the recorder if you want.

Monitoring and Viewing

Accessing live video feeds via computer, smartphone, or tablet In security Camera system

Using an app or client: Some security camera systems have their own apps or clients that you can install on your computer, smartphone, or tablet. These apps or clients allow you to view and control your cameras remotely. You need to sign in with your account credentials and connect your cameras to the app or client. For example, eufy Security app is a popular app for eufy security cameras.

Using a web browser: Some security camera systems offer web-based interfaces that allow you to access and control your cameras through a web browser. You need to find the IP address of your camera and enter it in the browser's address bar. You may also need to change the port forwarding settings on your router to allow the data from your camera to reach your device. For example, IP Webcam is a free Android app that turns your phone into a network camera that can be viewed from a web browser.

Using a third-party service: Some security camera systems support third-party services that enable you to view and store your camera footage online. These services usually require a subscription fee and may offer additional features such as cloud storage, motion detection, and alerts. For example, Ivideon is a cloud-based service that works with various types of cameras and devices.

Exploring different viewing options (local, remote, mobile apps) In security Camera system

There are different ways to explore the viewing options for your security camera system, depending on the type and model of your system. Here are some general steps you can follow:

Local viewing: This means viewing your cameras on a monitor or TV that is connected directly to your recorder (DVR or NVR). You can use the HDMI or VGA ports on the recorder to connect it to a monitor or TV. You can also use a mouse to navigate the recorder's menu and settings. You can switch between different camera views, playback recorded footage, adjust camera settings, and more.

Remote viewing: This means viewing your cameras on a device that is not connected to your recorder, such as a computer, smartphone, or tablet. You can use the internet to access your cameras from anywhere in the world. You need to set up some network configurations on your recorder and router, such as port forwarding and DDNS. You also need to download and install the app or software that is compatible with your system. You can use the app or software to view live and recorded video, control PTZ cameras, receive alerts, and more.

Mobile apps: These are apps that you can install on your smartphone or tablet to view your cameras remotely. They are usually free and easy to use. You need to scan the QR code or enter the serial number of your recorder to add your system to the app. You can also add multiple systems to the same app if you have more than one location. You can use the app to view live and recorded video, control PTZ cameras, receive alerts, and more.

Managing multiple cameras and camera groups In security Camera system

Managing multiple cameras and camera groups in a security camera system can help you organize and monitor your cameras more easily. Different security camera systems may have different ways to create and manage camera groups, but here are some common steps you can follow:

Find the camera group feature: Depending on your system, you may need to access the camera group feature from a web browser, an app, a software, or a recorder. For example, if you are using Synology Surveillance Station, you can go to Management > IP Camera > Group1
. If you are using Wyze cameras, you can use the Wyze app to create device groups.

Create a camera group: You can name your camera group and select the cameras you want to include in it. You can also create multiple camera groups for different purposes or locations. For example, you can create a group for indoor cameras and another group for outdoor cameras. You can also edit or delete your camera groups as needed.

View and control your camera group: Once you have created your camera group, you can view and control your cameras in the group from your device. You can switch between different camera views, playback recorded footage, adjust camera settings, and more. You can also grant user privileges to your camera group if you want to share the access with others.

Playback and review of recorded footage in In security Camera system

To playback and review recorded footage in a security camera system, you need to access the recorder (DVR or NVR) that stores the video data. There are different ways to access the recorder, such as using a monitor, a web browser, an app, or a software. Here are some general steps you can follow:

Using a monitor: You can connect a monitor or TV to your recorder using HDMI or VGA cables. You can also use a mouse to navigate the recorder's menu and settings. You can find the playback option, usually represented by a play icon, and select the channel, date, and time you want to review. You can use the playback controls to play, pause, fast forward, rewind, or zoom in the video. You can also export the video to a USB drive if you want to save it.

Using a web browser: You can access your recorder from a web browser on your computer or laptop. You need to find the IP address of your recorder and enter it in the browser's address bar. You may also need to change some network settings on your recorder and router, such as port forwarding and DDNS. You can log in with your username and password and access the web interface of your recorder. You can find the playback option and select the channel, date, and time you want to review. You can use the playback controls to play, pause, fast forward, rewind, or zoom in the video. You can also download the video to your computer if you want to save it.

Using an app or software: You can access your recorder from an app on your smartphone or tablet, or a software on your computer or laptop. You need to download and install the app or software that is compatible with your recorder. You can scan the QR code or enter the serial number of your recorder to add it to the app or software. You can log in with your username and password and access the interface of your recorder. You can find the playback option and select the channel, date, and time you want to review. You can use the playback controls to play, pause, fast forward, rewind, or zoom in the video. You can also share the video to other apps or devices if you want to save it.

Advanced Features and Integration

How to Explore Advanced Features in Security Camera Systems

Security camera systems are not just for recording video footage of what happens in your premises. They can also offer various advanced features that can enhance your security, convenience, and efficiency. Some of these features are:

Facial recognition: This feature allows your security camera to identify specific individuals by comparing their faces with a database of known faces. You can use this feature to grant access to authorized people, monitor attendance, or alert you of intruders or suspicious activities.

Object detection: This feature allows your security camera to detect and classify different objects within the scene, such as vehicles, animals, or weapons. You can use this feature to track traffic, count objects, or detect dangerous situations.

Smart alerts: This feature allows your security camera to send you notifications when it detects certain events or conditions, such as motion, sound, temperature, or humidity. You can use this feature to stay informed of what is happening in your premises, or to take action when needed.

To explore these advanced features in your security camera system, you need to follow these steps:

Step 1: Choose a Suitable Security Camera System

Not all security camera systems have the same capabilities and features. You need to choose a system that meets your needs and preferences. Some factors to consider are:

The type of camera: There are different types of cameras, such as dome, bullet, PTZ, or wireless cameras. Each type has its own advantages and disadvantages, depending on the location, coverage, and installation of the camera.

The resolution and quality of the camera: The higher the resolution and quality of the camera, the clearer and sharper the images and videos it produces. This can affect the accuracy and performance of the advanced features, such as facial recognition and object detection.

The storage and connectivity of the camera: The storage and connectivity of the camera determine how you can access and manage the data and features of the camera. You can choose between cloud-based or local storage, and between wired or wireless connectivity.

The compatibility and integration of the camera: The compatibility and integration of the camera determine how well it works with other devices and systems, such as your smartphone, computer, or smart home devices. You can choose a camera that supports common standards and protocols, such as Wi-Fi, Bluetooth, or ONVIF.

Step 2: Install and Configure Your Security Camera System

Once you have chosen a suitable security camera system, you need to install and configure it properly. Some tips to follow are:

Follow the instructions and guidelines provided by the manufacturer or the installer of the camera system. Make sure you have all the necessary tools and equipment, such as screws, cables, or power adapters.

Choose a strategic location and angle for your camera, where it can capture a clear and wide view of the area you want to monitor. Avoid placing the camera in direct sunlight, glare, or shadows, as this can affect the quality and visibility of the images and videos.

Connect your camera to a reliable power source and a stable network. Test the connection and the functionality of the camera before proceeding to the next step.

Download and install the app or software that comes with your camera system, or use a compatible third-party app or software. This will allow you to access and control the features and settings of your camera from your smartphone, computer, or other devices.

Step 3: Enable and Customize the Advanced Features of Your Security Camera System

After installing and configuring your security camera system, you can enable and customize the advanced features that you want to use. Some steps to follow are:

Facial recognition: To use this feature, you need to create a database of known faces that you want your camera to recognize. You can do this by uploading photos or videos of the individuals, or by capturing their faces using the camera. You can also assign names, labels, or groups to the faces, and set different actions or rules for each face, such as allowing or denying access, sending alerts, or triggering other devices.

Object detection: To use this feature, you need to select the types of objects that you want your camera to detect and classify. You can choose from predefined categories, such as vehicles, animals, or weapons, or create your own custom categories. You can also set different actions or rules for each object, such as counting, tracking, or sending alerts.

Smart alerts: To use this feature, you need to select the events or conditions that you want your camera to notify you of. You can choose from predefined options, such as motion, sound, temperature, or humidity, or create your own custom options. You can also set different actions or rules for each alert, such as recording, playing a sound, or triggering other devices.

Step 4: Monitor and Manage Your Security Camera System

After enabling and customizing the advanced features of your security camera system, you can monitor and manage your system using the app or software that you installed in step 2. Some functions that you can perform are:

View live or recorded video footage from your camera, and zoom, pan, or tilt the camera if it supports these functions.

Receive and review the alerts and notifications from your camera, and take appropriate actions if needed.

Adjust the settings and preferences of your camera and its features, such as the sensitivity, frequency, or duration of the features.

Update the firmware and software of your camera and its features, to ensure optimal performance and security.

Integrating the security camera system with other smart home devices

Integrating the security camera system with other smart home devices can make your home more convenient, secure, and efficient. You can use a voice assistant, a smarthome hub, or a dedicated tablet to control all your devices from one place.

Here are some suggestions for accomplishing that:

Voice assistant: You can use a voice assistant, such as Google Home, Amazon Alexa, or Apple Siri, to communicate with your security camera system and other smart home devices using voice commands. For example, you can say "Hey Google, show me the front door camera" or "Alexa, turn on the porch light". To use this option, you need to make sure that your security camera system and other devices are compatible with the voice assistant you choose, and that you have set up the proper accounts and skills to link them together.

Smarthome hub: You can use a smarthome hub, such as Samsung SmartThings, Wink, or Hubitat, to connect and manage your security camera system and other smart home devices using a single app or web interface. For example, you can create routines, scenes, or automations that trigger your devices based on certain conditions or events. To use this option, you need to make sure that your security camera system and other devices are compatible with the smarthome hub you choose, and that you have followed the instructions to pair them with the hub.

Dedicated tablet: You can use a dedicated tablet, such as an iPad, an Android tablet, or a Kindle Fire, to display and control your security camera system and other smart home devices using a customized dashboard or interface. For example, you can use apps like ActionTiles, Home Assistant, or ImperiHome to create your own smarthome dashboard that shows the live video feeds from your cameras, the status of your devices, and the buttons or sliders to control them. To use this option, you need to make sure that your security camera system and other devices are compatible with the app you choose, and that you have configured the app to access and control them.

Setting up notifications and alerts for motion detection or specific events

Setting up notifications and alerts for motion detection or specific events in security camera systems can help you stay informed and alert of what is happening in your premises. Depending on the type and model of your security camera system, the steps to set up notifications and alerts may vary. However, Here are some broad steps you can adhere to:

Enable or reconfigure motion detection: You need to enable the motion detection feature on your security camera system, and adjust the sensitivity, frequency, and area of the motion detection according to your needs. You can also create motion zones or schedules to limit the motion detection to certain times or areas.

Set up the push notifications on the phone app: You need to download and install the app that is compatible with your security camera system, and enable the push notifications on your phone settings. You can also customize the notification sound, vibration, and display options on the app settings.

Update the firmware and software: You need to make sure that your security camera system and the app are updated to the latest firmware and software versions, to ensure optimal performance and security. You can check for updates on the app or the web interface of your security camera system, and follow the instructions to install them.

Change cameras' placement: You need to make sure that your cameras are placed in strategic locations and angles, where they can capture a clear and wide view of the area you want to monitor. You should also avoid placing the cameras in direct sunlight, glare, or shadows, as this can affect the quality and visibility of the images and videos

Troubleshooting and Maintenance

Power and connection problems: Sometimes, security cameras may not receive enough power or have a stable network connection, which can affect their performance. To fix this, you can check the power source, the cables, the PoE switch, the router, and the network settings of your cameras.

Image quality problems: Security cameras may produce blurry, grainy, or distorted images due to various reasons, such as dirty lens, low resolution, poor lighting, varifocal zoom issues, or WiFi interference. To fix this, you can clean the lens, adjust the resolution, improve the lighting, calibrate the zoom, or change the WiFi channel.

IP conflict problems: Security cameras may have the same IP address as other devices on the same network, which can cause network errors and prevent the cameras from working properly. To fix this, you can change the IP address of your cameras manually or use DHCP to assign them automatically.

Software and firmware problems: Security cameras may have outdated or incompatible software or firmware, which can cause bugs, glitches, or security vulnerabilities. To fix this, you can update the software and firmware of your cameras regularly or reset them to factory settings.

Regular maintenance tasks (cleaning, firmware updates, etc.)

Regular maintenance tasks are important to keep your security camera system functioning properly and protecting your property. Some of the common tasks that you can do yourself or with the help of a professional service are:

Cleaning: You should clean the camera lens, casing, and wiring regularly to remove any dust, dirt, or debris that may affect the image quality or damage the equipment. You can use a can of compressed air, a microfibre cloth, and a weak cleaning solution to gently wipe the surfaces.

Firmware updates: You should update the firmware of your cameras and other devices regularly to fix any bugs, improve performance, and enhance security. You can check the manufacturer's website or app for the latest firmware versions and follow the instructions to install them.

Cable management: You should check the cables and connectors of your cameras and other devices for any wear and tear, loose wires, or exposed wires that may cause power or network problems. You can replace any damaged cables or connectors and use cable ties or clips to organize them neatly.

Calibration: You should check the camera view, resolution, zoom, pan, tilt, and motion detection settings and adjust them as needed to ensure that you can see your property perimeter clearly and capture the details you want. You can use your controller, monitor, or app to change the settings and test the functions.

Power management: You should check the power source, PoE switch, and battery backup of your cameras and other devices and make sure that they are working properly and providing enough power. You can test the voltage, current, and continuity of the circuits and replace any faulty components.

Speaker/microphone maintenance: You should check the speakers and microphones of your cameras and other devices and make sure that they are working properly and transmitting clear sound. You can test the audio quality, volume, and feedback of the devices and adjust them as needed.

Remote control testing: You should check the remote control or app of your cameras and other devices and make sure that they are working properly and communicating with the devices. You can test the buttons, functions, and commands of the remote control or app and update them as needed.

How to Contacting customer support for further assistance

If you need further assistance with your security camera system, you can contact the customer support of the manufacturer or the service provider of your system. Depending on the brand and model of your system, you may have different options to contact them, such as phone, email, chat, or online form. Here are some examples of how to contact customer support for some popular security camera brands:

Honeywell Home: You can call 1-888-425-6739 and select option 2 for technical support, or chat with a specialist online by selecting the Help option in the bottom right side of your browser screen. You can also visit their support page for more information and resources.

Lorex: You can call 1-888-425-6739 and select option 2 for technical support, or chat with a representative online by visiting their support page. You can also find manuals, downloads, videos, and FAQs on their website.

CCTV Camera World: You can call (716) 229-0080 or pre-purchase a session online by visiting their support page. You can also find guides, tutorials, and videos on their website.

Night Owl: You can chat with a technical support representative online by selecting the Help option in the bottom right side of your browser screen. You can also visit their support page for more information and resources.

Defender: You can submit a support case online by filling out a form on their contact page. You can also find manuals, downloads, videos, and FAQs on their website

FAQs

What advantages does a security camera system offer? A security camera system can provide many benefits for home and business owners, such as:

- **Enhancing security and deterring crime**
- **Monitoring activities and events**
- **Providing evidence and documentation**
- **Improving productivity and efficiency**
- **Reducing insurance costs and liability risks**

What types of security cameras are available and what are the differences between them? There are various types of security cameras, such as:

Analog cameras: These cameras use coaxial cables to transmit video signals to a DVR (digital video recorder). They are typically cheaper and easier to install, but have lower resolution and quality than digital cameras.

IP cameras: These cameras use Ethernet cables or Wi-Fi to transmit video signals to a NVR (network video recorder) or a cloud server. They offer higher resolution and quality, as well as more features and flexibility, than analog cameras.

Wireless cameras: These cameras use batteries and Wi-Fi to transmit video signals to a NVR or a cloud server. They are convenient and portable, but require frequent battery changes and may have signal interference issues.

Wired cameras: These cameras use power and data cables to transmit video signals to a DVR or a NVR.

They are more reliable and secure, but require professional installation and may have limited placement options.

How do I choose the best security camera system for my needs? There are several factors to consider when choosing a security camera system, such as:

Budget: The cost of a security camera system depends on the number, type, and quality of the cameras, as well as the storage and monitoring options. You should compare the features and benefits of different systems and choose the one that suits your budget and needs.

Location: The location of the cameras determines the coverage, lighting, and weather conditions. You should choose the cameras that can work well in different environments, such as indoor or outdoor, day or night, sunny or rainy, etc.

Purpose: The purpose of the cameras determines the resolution, angle, and zoom of the cameras. You should choose the cameras that can capture the details and activities that you want to monitor, such as faces, license plates, movements, etc.

Integration: The integration of the cameras determines the compatibility and functionality of the cameras. You should choose the cameras that can work with your existing systems, such as alarm, intercom, smart home, etc., as well as offer remote access and control via mobile devices or web browsers.

How do I install and maintain a security camera system? The installation and maintenance of a security camera system depend on the type and complexity of the system. You may need to hire a professional installer or do it yourself, depending on your skills and preferences. Some general steps are:

- **Plan the layout and placement of the cameras and wires**
- **Mount the cameras and connect the wires to the power and data sources**
- **Set up the DVR or NVR and configure the settings and preferences**

Evaluate the system and make any necessary adjustments.

Regularly check the system and replace the batteries, cables, or cameras if damaged or malfunctioning.